Images of

THE GAMBLE HOUSE

Masterwork of Greene & Greene

Jeanette A. Thomas

Photography by

Theodore Thomas with Kuniko Okubo

Balcony Press
Los Angeles

This book is dedicated to the memory of Charles and Henry Greene,
and David and Mary Gamble who created The House;
to the heirs of Cecil and Louise Gamble who assured its preservation; and its Director Emeritus,
Randell L. Makinson, whose perception and scholarship have shown us how to see it.

IMAGES OF THE GAMBLE HOUSE: Masterwork of Greene and Greene
©1989 University of Southern California
Published in the United States of America 1994 by Balcony Press
Printed in Hong Kong
No part of this book may be reproduced in any manner without written permission except in the
case of brief quotations embodied in critical articles and reviews.
For information, address Balcony Press, 2690 Locksley Place, Los Angeles, California 90039
Cover photo: Headboard in Master Bedroom by Peter Shamray

Library of Congress Catalog Card Number: 94-072621
ISBN 0-9643119-1-7

Contents

Garage Door Detail

𝒯he Gamble House at Dusk

*𝒯he idea was to eliminate everything unnecessary,
to make the whole as direct and as simple as possible
but always with the beautiful in mind as the final goal.*

Henry Mather Greene

The evolution of a house

Charles Sumner Greene

Henry Mather Greene [1]

The year was 1907 and all was right with the world. It was a time of confidence and hope. Theodore Roosevelt, in the last year of his presidency, typified the exuberance and energy of the nation. Even before the Panama Canal was completed, he sent the United States Fleet around the world in a bold show of strength and a bid for global peace.

Plumbing, electricity, the automobile, and the airplane were becoming part of daily life. Four years earlier, in 1903, an advertisement for a shower bath appeared, the long distance telephone reached from New York to Omaha, two men drove their Packard from San Francisco to New York in fifty-two days, and the Wright brothers stayed aloft for nearly a minute over the beaches of Kitty Hawk in their power-driven airplane. At the St. Louis Fair of 1904, people were delighted with the demonstration of new inventions like the electrical hearing aid and the vacuum cleaner that were sure to improve the quality of life. Even glaring social problems like child labor were approached with the assurance that wrongs could be corrected. People were convinced they could control their destiny; everything was possible.

Pasadena, California, had begun as an agricultural community, the Indiana Colony, in 1873. By 1886 it had grown large enough to

incorporate as a town and new resort hotels were soon built to take advantage of the beautiful surroundings and ideal climate. Guests from the East often came almost to the hotel doors in their own private railroad cars. Among the rich and famous who stayed in these hostelries were Theodore Roosevelt, Andrew Carnegie, and Charlie Chaplin. Pasadena became the premier winter resort of the area. Before long, it became a city of fine homes built by hotel patrons who had decided to stay. It also became a city of talented architects.

The brothers Charles Sumner Greene and Henry Mather Greene were in the most productive period of their careers when they met David and Mary Gamble in 1907. As architects, they were in the enviable position of having attracted an impressive list of wealthy clients who commissioned them to design fine homes, granting generous budgets and a relatively free rein. The commissions included not only the buildings but their grounds and interior furnishings, for this was the height of the Craftsman Period when a unified domestic setting was the esthetic goal. Even furniture maker Gustav Stickley began to plan houses because he realized that traditional dwellings were incompatible with his starkly plain Craftsman furniture. The concept of total design had been stressed in the German rooms at the 1904 Louisiana Purchase International Exposition in St. Louis. Architects like Frank Lloyd Wright and the Greenes included the complete environment when developing a project.

The dominant difference between the work of Wright and the Greenes, however, lay in what each considered to be the essential nature of architecture. For Wright it was geometric space, for the Greenes it was craftsmanship. Because of their early training, Charles and Henry Greene looked upon architecture from the perspective of the master craftsman.

1. Photos courtesy of the Greene and Greene Library

Dr. Thomas Greene, their father, was a friend of Calvin Milton Woodward, founder of the Manual Training High School, operated by Washington University in St. Louis, Missouri. The boys were enrolled in Woodward's innovative school and their experiences there affected the kind of architects they would become. Along with academic studies the curriculum included three years of shop training where one year was devoted to woodworking, another year to metal working, and a final year to machine tool design. Woodward's goals were nonvocational. He found that when students developed their manual skills, they could build models which helped in understanding the formulas and principals of mechanics that he was trying to teach. Calvin Woodward wanted to educate "the whole boy"; it was his conviction that the well-educated man should work with his hands as well as his mind.

In 1888, Charles and Henry Greene entered the School of Architecture at Boston Tech (later to become part of the Massachusetts Institute of Technology), where their training was in the tradition of historic European styles. They stayed on in Boston working in architectural offices, and came to Pasadena in 1893 to visit their parents who had moved west for Mrs. Greene's health. The young men were attracted to the area and soon decided to establish their own architectural firm in this new community. Their first commission was for a tombstone, the second was a modest house for a friend of their father. The early projects reflected the traditional tastes of their clients, but in time, Greene and Greene achieved recognition for developing the California bungalow to a high art and for creating houses with the quality of fine furniture.

The term, architect, comes from the Greek words *arkos* and *tekton*, meaning chief worker; originally, the architect was a **master builder**. The role has changed through the years, however, from that of the highly skilled artisan who developed a Gothic cathedral, to that of the artist or engineer who designs a project and then turns it over to a contractor for construction. From this perspective, Frank Lloyd Wright once asked Charles Greene how he achieved the rare quality of workmanship in his houses. Although his answer is not recorded, Greene's words quoted by Elmer Gray in the October, 1922 issue of *Architectural Record* were appropriate. (pp. 310, 315) "Here is the difference; prevailing custom is a system of administration by recorded instruction; mine is not *any* system, but personal direction on the job. The first is fixed, the second is elastic, yielding to contingencies, open to inspiration." A comparison of blueprints with the finished house shows this to be true. Often they appear to be a point of departure rather than a set of instructions.

Even though their contractor, Peter Hall, was a master craftsman with a well trained crew of carpenters, Henry Greene or his brother was at the building site regularly. If something was not right it was torn out and done again. Charles Greene was also involved daily at Hall's carpentry shop where he worked with the cabinetmakers who were under the supervision of John Hall, Peter's talented brother. John Hall's skill and knowledge as a master craftsman had an important influence on the designs of Charles Greene's furniture.

The brothers Greene were able to create their unique houses because they combined the skill of the craftsman with the vision of the artist. Charles described the role of his profession in its original sense when he wrote, "An architect is a builder employing the process of art." (*The Architect*, "Architecture as a Fine Art", April, 1917, p. 218.)

It should be added, however, that the passion for expert craftsmanship ultimately limited their practice. This was an extraordinary period, but the magic of the years "after plumbing and before taxes" was destined to run out. The unwillingness of Greene and Greene to meet the realities of the changing economic picture meant that they priced themselves out of the market. By 1916, most of their major work was done. Frank Lloyd Wright, in contrast, was professionally active until his death in 1959.

Mr. and Mrs. David B. Gamble were from Cincinnati, Ohio. Mr. Gamble, whose father had been one of the founders of the Proctor and Gamble Company, had retired in 1895 but remained active with the firm as a member of the board of directors. In the winter when his sons were in school, he and his wife, Mary, would escape the cold weather by spending four or five months at the Raymond Hotel in South Pasadena.

After only one meeting with their prospective patrons from Ohio, the Greenes were engaged to design a house on Westmoreland Place. It was to be a permanent residence for David and Mary Gamble and Julia Huggins, Mrs. Gamble's maiden sister. The eldest of their three sons had just married and the two younger boys were away at school during the academic year. David Gamble lived until 1923, his widow until 1929. Miss Huggins had the distinction of residing in the house longer than any of the Gambles; she was there until her death in 1945.

By great good fortune, the next residents were the Gamble's eldest son, Cecil, and his wife, Louise, who recognized the architectural importance of their home and maintained it without major changes. In 1966 their heirs presented the property to the City of Pasadena in a joint agreement with The University of Southern California. Because ownership continued in the family from 1908-1966, the house was never remodeled, the beautiful interior woods were never painted,

and the furnishings remained intact. The structure may be seen today as it was originally designed.

The Gamble House was a radical change from the opulent mansions built in Pasadena at the turn of the century. Rather than imitating the classical buildings of Europe, it represented an American style well-suited to the southern California climate. Long recognized as one of the most significant houses in the United States, it has had a profound impact on residential architecture.

By the mid nineteenth century, some architects were turning away from the monumental, historic styles to one that was simpler, more functional and related to the needs of people. They were part of the Arts and Crafts Movement which began in England and spread to Europe and America. Leaders in this reform declared that dull, repetitive mill work led to shoddy goods and poor taste. Deploring the misery and ugliness stemming from the industrial revolution, they lauded the system of medieval guilds which gave the craftsman a sense of dignity and worth through his handiwork. Because the artisan designed and created a useful article from start to finish, he developed a sense of beauty and of pride; the machine, in contrast, separated the worker from his craft, diminishing his sense of accomplishment. The Arts and Crafts Movement made an important contribution to architecture and interior design when it simplified houses and their furnishings, promoted handcrafted articles in place of machine-made copies that were popular during the Victorian Period, and encouraged interaction with nature to offset some of the degrading effects of the machine.

The Gamble House, through its functional approach and superb craftsmanship, demonstrates the main tenets of the Arts and Crafts Movement. Many practical elements reflect the common sense and ingenuity of the period. Ceiling vents in interior closets promote the circulation of air. Oval, rather than round poles, for clothes hangers in the wardrobes provide added strength to prevent sagging. Entrance from the kitchen to the pantry is less crowded because the angle at the corner of a pantry cabinet and counter top has been widened. Rain gutters are an integral part of the roof so they do not mar the roof line. A system of underground drainage pipes carries rainwater from the downspouts to the streets at the front and rear of the property.

Every Craftsman house was sure to have some built-in furniture. Buffets, cabinets, open shelves, bookcases, chests of drawers, wardrobe closets, benches, window seats and, of course, medicine cabinets. The more expensive the house, the more built-ins there would be. The rooms and closets of The Gamble House contain every variety of beautifully crafted, functional, built-in furniture.

This is a house of wood where articulated joinery becomes a decorative feature both inside and out. Rounded edges create sculpted forms wherever two pieces of wood are joined. In fact, every post and lintel, rail and beam has been softened by hand sanding; not a single member is left as it came from the mill. Edges of the fireplace bricks are also rounded to continue the effect. Mundane details like foundation vents, drain pipes, chimneys, garage doors, and light switch plates have been designed to combine utility and beauty in each object.

Like other Arts and Crafts designers, the Greenes borrowed from the native arts and architecture of both Europe and Japan. European strains are reflected in the cantilevered second story over the front terrace, window boxes and shingles on exterior walls, the long roof lines and Swiss-like exterior elevation south of the front door, the living room inglenook, and the Gothic fireplace in the den.

The floor plan, which may represent a preference of the owners, suggests European formality. Spaces are welcoming and gracious, yet privacy seems to be an overriding concern. Every room in the house, with the exception of the living room, can be closed off with a door (the kitchen has five doors!), and a wide central corridor divides rooms from each other both upstairs and down. A short passage separates Mr. Gamble's den from the front hall while the guest suite and the kitchen are secluded by small entryways with a door at each end. On the second floor, family bedrooms and a guest room are set apart in the four corners of the house. Quarters for the staff are isolated by an L shaped hall leading to the maids' rooms and bath.

Widespread interest in things Japanese had been fostered by the Philadelphia Centennial Exposition of 1876; with the World's Colombian Exposition in Chicago in 1893, oriental influences quickly found their way into the domestic architecture of the Western World. An emphasis on the horizontal line, the use of modular units, a taste for the asymmetrical, the absence of clutter and nicknacks, extensive areas of unpainted wood, a preponderance of natural and subdued colors, a close relationship with the outdoors, all are elements from Japan that were incorporated into the Craftsman style. Charles and Henry Greene had acquired a remarkable knowledge and understanding of the art and architecture of that region, although they had never traveled to the Orient. Their information came from studying books and pictures and by their visit to the Japanese pavilion at the Chicago fair on their way to California in 1893.

Japanese identification with nature is so strong that a dwelling and its immediate surroundings are thought of as one structure. That concept also appears on the sleeping porches and broad terraces of The Gamble House. These spaces integrate the building with the garden, but they are also an extension of adjacent rooms; the same materials and details that are used inside appear on the walls and posts of sleeping porch and terrace, affirming, "This, too, is a living space."

Living in rapport with nature inspires the interior design, as well. Flowers and trees described in leaded art glass are found in doors, windows, and lanterns; furniture is inlaid with patterns of the iris, dogwood, and a trailing rose; fireplaces are decorated with flowers of Tiffany glass; stylized trees appear in specially woven rugs; redwood panels surrounding the upper walls of the living room are carved with trees, clouds, birds, and the Chinese symbol of good fortune: bats.

These panels are similar to a feature of the Japanese house where the door lintel runs the entire length of a room to accommodate the sliding screens forming a partition. The space between this beam and the ceiling is called the *ramma* (pronounced with an "L"). Sometimes the *ramma* is filled in with plaster, other times it contains lattice work or a carved panel with open areas in the design. It was common, in Craftsman houses, to extend the door rail all the way around a room as a unifying detail. Often, it became a convenient picture rail.

Indigenous shapes from Japan appear throughout The Gamble House: the contour of the dining room table, the cloud lift in the transom bar of each window, the recessed handles in letter box drawers or the ebony framed pattern of negative space in the master bedroom furniture. Searching out the quiet presence of these graceful forms can be a rewarding treasure hunt.

In his book *The Hidden Dimension* (Doubleday, 1966) pp. 143-144, Edward T. Hall observed, "The study of Japanese spaces illustrates their habit of leading the individual to a spot where he can discover something for himself." This is a principle well expressed by the Greenes when stepping stones lead to a secluded bench in the garden; or the brick border on the back terrace becomes an inviting path along the edge of the fish pond; when the view from Aunt Julia's sleeping porch extends from the pond and terrace below, past the lawn and flowers as they merge with the treetops, to the distant hills in the background, and the entire vista becomes her "garden of borrowed scenery," a familiar landscape plan in Japan. These and countless other spots invite discovery.

A good house which satisfies the needs and desires of the people who live in it, requires a fruitful dialogue between a talented architect and an involved owner. It was almost certain that the David Gambles would receive a superior house because they knew what they wanted and were very active in the development of their home.

They chose not to construct a monument to themselves. The building site was on a small, private street rather than a wide thoroughfare where everyone who passed could admire the house. To preserve the rural atmosphere, the Gambles purchased five adjacent acres of orange groves to the west. They selected architects who were well known for designing "ultimate bungalows," an apt term used by Randell L. Makinson. These are large, expensive dwellings by Greene and Greene which shared the functional aspects of their smaller contemporaries and tended not to look as costly as they actually were. Mary Gamble wanted a house that related to the outdoors and would be suitable for occasional entertaining, one that would provide privacy for its occupants and comfortable quarters for guests. She asked that the interior design incorporate some of her cherished possessions: a bronze crane from the Orient, several Rookwood ceramic pieces, a fern bowl and lamp by Louis Comfort Tiffany.

David Gamble's preferences were reflected in the den. To accommodate his interest in business and civic affairs, four oak commercial file drawers were incorporated with oak cabinets built on either side of the fireplace. Although other furniture was designed for the room, ultimately, pieces from Mr. Gamble's Cincinnati study came to furnish his Pasadena den.

A series of preliminary pencil sketches[1] by the architects display the gradual progress toward plans that eventually suited the owners. Several improvements appeared in the kitchen: the sink and cook stove were moved to more efficient locations, ventilation was increased, the kitchen was lengthened to accommodate the center table, and the cold room was added. At the front of the house the guest suite lacked its big square closet, the bath was not compartmentalized, and the den was without a fireplace.

However, it was on the second floor that consultation with the owners brought the most dramatic revisions. Aunt Julia's sleeping porch was altered to bring indoor-outdoor living to the upstairs. Originally a small area off her bedroom, it was transformed into a spacious outdoor sitting room with additional access from the upstairs hall. This important change created a welcome source of light and air as the corridor was lengthened to extend the full width of the house. Further refinements increased the closet space in the family bedrooms and augmented the boys' room with a bath. (One can imagine Mary Gamble saying, "Even if they are not here much of the time, they should have their own bathroom.") They got it and with a stall shower made of marble!

The most significant addition of all involved the exceptional front elevation facing the street. In the first scheme, the structure ended with the boys' room; there was no sleeping porch or *balcony*, as it was designated on the blueprints. Consequently, the dominating horizontal line of the second story would have been shortened and the expansive overhang of the porch roof, like a broad umbrella, would not have been part of this remarkable facade. The light, open feeling under the roof provides an agreeable contrast with the vertical mass at the opposite end of the building. This singular area of negative space, accented by the distinctive texture of the porch railing, sets The Gamble House apart.

With the notable gifts of Charles and Henry Greene and the perceptive suggestions of the Gambles, the house evolved to meet the owners' needs and surpass the early plans. Fortunately, this crucial interaction between architect and patron was also complimented by the period and the place; all were decisive collaborators in the work of art that we admire today.

1. From The Greene and Greene Library.

Themes in The Gamble House

*The whole construction was carefully thought
out and there was a reason for every detail.*

Henry Mather Greene

Much of the beauty in The Gamble House derives from hundreds of details that appear both inside and out. From the chevron pattern in the circular brick driveway to the ceramic planters on the terrace, from the hand-shaped rafter tails to the unique window screens, every aspect of the exterior contributes to the overall scheme. Inside of the house the furniture, picture frames, light fixtures, stained glass windows, and fireplace tiles are a part of the total design. Separate elements are coordinated by the use of patterns and motifs which reappear in varied forms and materials.

This artful arrangement of parts is like a musical composition that states a theme which is repeated many times, always with a different treatment. The Greenes, composing with the materials of architecture, created a masterpiece of theme and variations.

Following are selected views of these many details arranged into eight themes which recur throughout the house and garden.

*W*ide terraces connect the house
with its surroundings. These are
garden rooms, roofed by the
sleeping porches above.

I. TRANSITION
A Theme That Signals Change

*When one approaches such a house it must not
obtrude itself upon one's sight but rather fit into
things about it.*

Charles Sumner Greene

There is a natural, welcoming atmosphere about The Gamble House; proportions are generous, textures are rich, and the undisguised surfaces of materials are featured. Many well considered elements relate the house to its surroundings. Rafters extending beyond the broad eaves are softened along the edges and at the ends to correspond with the rounded shapes in nature; native boulders are massed at the bottom of a brick wall and smaller stones appear among the bricks so that natural and man-made materials blend with each other; green lawns spread up to the terrace wall where vines become a part of the building; the whole structure seems to grow from the land surrounding it.

Interior spaces continue a theme of gradual change: a short passageway provides a transition between entry hall and guest room, a brick wall arches before it meets the ceiling beams, a rosebush is abstracted in an exterior window. The atmosphere is one of continuity, unhurried and gracious.

I. Transition: Sleeping porch detail

$\mathcal{D}$riveway, planting and

house present a unified design.

*T*he bricks change in texture,

size and color when the driveway

and the landing meet.

A gnarled oak tree of leaded glass

sustains a transition from exterior

to interior. The contrast between

shingled walls and teak doors hints

at the elegance inside.

*T*wo inviting paths:
one of pressed brick
curves toward the
edge of the pond,
the other of river stone
leads into the garden.

A terrace wall of clinker brick and
fieldstone integrates building and site.

*C*linker bricks develop irregular
shapes and colors when they are
near the heat source in the kiln.
Some resemble lava and seem more
natural than man-made.

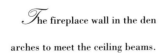
A view from Aunt Julia's room toward the sleeping porch, a transition to the out of doors.

The fireplace wall in the den arches to meet the ceiling beams.

A gradual change in ceiling
height is achieved by revealing
the underside of the stairs.

𝒯he lowest step

fans out toward the wall.

$\mathscr{T}$wo views of the dining room
window. The abstraction in leaded
art glass and the nearby rosebush
mirror one another, blending
nature and art.

II. JOINERY
Expressing Form and Function

*It may be only a sheltered nook with a cozy
seat...sawed and hammered and pegged...
with the passion that makes beauty grow.*

Charles Sumner Greene

The Gamble House displays the Greenes' deep respect for wood. Seventeen different varieties with varying colors and grains appear in the house and its furnishings. The materials were carefully selected and the special attributes of each piece considered in its use.

The beauty of the wood was enhanced as joinery became an essential element of design. The architects were sensitive to the textures and patterns inherent in an open mortise and tenon joint at the corner of a drawer, a mantle piece, a baseboard, or a step. Repeatedly, the dark end-grain of a projecting tenon appears in contrast with the long smooth grain of the member containing an open mortise. The rounded corners create a sculptural quality; shapes are emphasized when sanded edges produce a shadow line between adjacent pieces.

Charles and Henry Greene were unsurpassed in developing beautiful designs through joinery. They were true representatives of the Craftsman Movement, bringing further integrity to their work because the appearance of an object was inspired by its function.

II. Joinery: *D*riveway detail

$\mathscr{A}$ teak beam in the entry hall

is sculpted to fit the sanded

corner of a mahogany block.

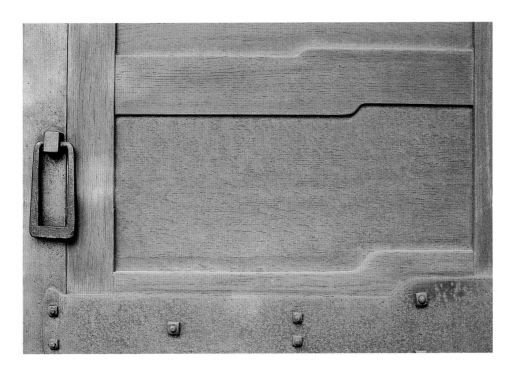

*C*reative use of nuts and bolts
joins wrought iron with oak
in the unusual garage doors.

*T*hird floor wall detail.
Panels of Port Orford cedar
contrast with the active pattern
of Douglas fir; functional dowels
add interest to the design.

In the kitchen, a maple scarf joint with

oak blocks locking it together.

Detail of wall and ceiling in the upstairs

guest room. The scarf joint creates a

unique pattern as it splices together

sections of the door-height rail.

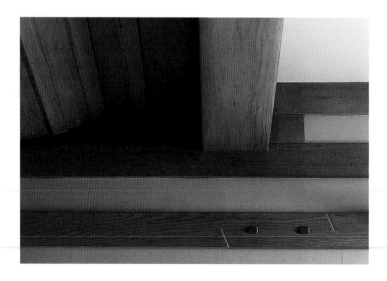

*I*ndirect lighting fixtures of

cedar hang from leather straps

in the master bedroom.

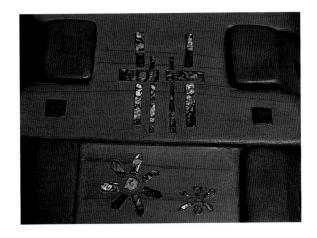

*J*oinery detail on hanging cedar

light with inlay of abalone.

*S*teel straps with wedges surround corbels

supporting the top flight of the stairway.

*W*rought iron straps and wedges create

a functional design with the attic beams.

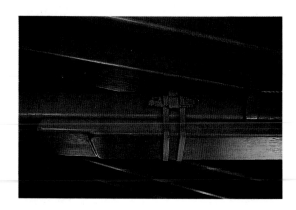

$\mathcal{T}$he extension mechanism of the

dining table forms a pattern like a

Japanese puzzle.

Teak staircase wall and bannister in the entry

hall. Each horizontal board forms the side of a

step; the hand rail creates a rhythmic pattern

matching the risers and treads of the stairs.

III. ORIENTAL FORMS
A Unifying Thread

Thus it may be seen that in a work of art as in a piece of tapestry, the same thread runs through the web, but goes to make up different figures.

Charles Sumner Greene

A general interest in the Eastern world was widespread in Europe and America long before the turn of the century. Travel to the Orient was gaining in popularity and the paintings of French Impressionists reflected their admiration of Japanese woodblock prints which many of these artists collected. The Arts and Crafts Movement was also greatly influenced by the art and architecture of Japan.

In The Gamble House, the most widely used pattern from the Orient is an abstraction of clouds or mist. All of the exterior doors, windows and screens are divided with a transom bar that rises to a slightly higher plane across the center of the opening and returns to the original level. This is a figure typically found in the supporting rails of Chinese tables. Charles Greene also employed the oriental lift to taper a beam, shape the arm of a chair, or compose the leaded pattern in a lantern.

Several other shapes which are indigenous to Japan inspired the design of light switch plates, drawer handles, and even the dining table. Invariably, forms found in nature are the inspiration for these patterns.

III. Oriental Forms: *Living* room truss and ramma detail

The cloud abstraction appears as a

geometric pattern on an exterior lantern.

This copper lantern with an oriental shape has developed

a fine patina from long exposure to the weather.

*T*he sculpted end of the built-in
seat in the master bedroom.

*E*ach exterior window exhibits
the oriental lift and a western
pattern of the sun's rays.

*T*he arm of an inglenook

bench in the living room.

*D*rawer pulls and silver handle on the maple

desk in the guest room derived from Japanese

design.

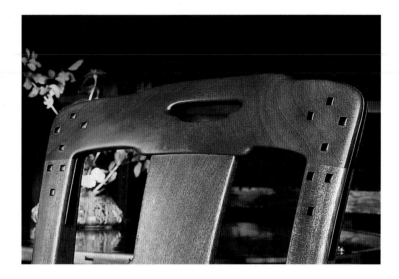

*D*etail of dining room chair.

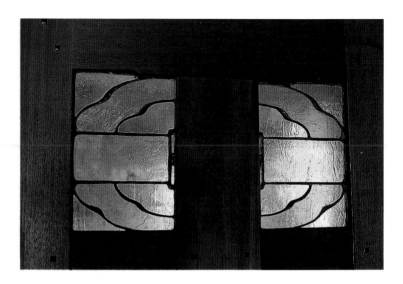

*T*he leaded art glass in a dining room door

describes the shape of the extended dining table.

A headboard in the master bedroom.

The ebony shapes and asymmetrical

composition are intrinsic to Japan.

$\mathcal{L}$antern and ceiling plate in the upstairs hall.

The rose and crane from the Gamble family crest

are featured with contours from Japan.

$\mathcal{W}$indow of borrowed light, looking from the

master bedroom toward the upstairs hall.

IV. THE THEME OF THREE

An Aspect of the Mind

*The division of a composition into three
related parts is...universal.*

Charles Sumner Greene

Charles Greene's fascination with the use of three components can be seen in every room. He featured triple forms in grouping drawers, designing furniture, or tapering a king post. Sometimes the parts are symmetrically arranged, frequently they are not. The Gamble House reflects a taste for oriental asymmetry as often as a preference for classical balance. The structure fits in with nature which welcomes a variety of proportions. The Theme of Three is an esthetic principle which inspired some of the most interesting of Charles Greene's designs.

IV. Theme of Three: *Den* fireplace wall

$\mathcal{D}$etail of king post truss on the third floor.

Originally planned for billiards, this room became

the most beautiful attic in Pasadena because of

Mr. Gamble's lack of interest in the game.

$\mathcal{D}$etail of inglenook in the living room. The corbel

and beams provide another variation on the trine.

$\mathcal{T}$hree planes are carved into the post

of the living room mantle; the corner

joinery continues the theme.

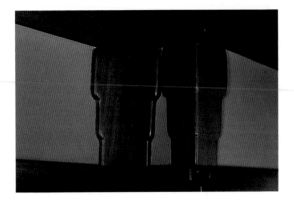

This mahogany detail in the dining room occurs
where there are structural posts within the wall.

The baseboard rises in a triad to meet the bottom step in the entry
hall; joinery at the corner of the steps repeats a familiar pattern.

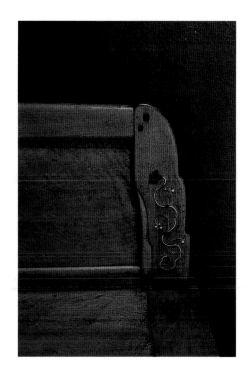

Detail on the maple desk in the first floor guest room. A graceful rhythm borrowed from Japan is expressed in wood.

Detail of guest room chair. The leg joins a three level pattern carved in the rocker.

The solid maple table in the kitchen with its trio of drawers which extend all the way through from one side to the other to balance the weight when they are opened.

A sconce on the master bedroom wall.

*T*he cedar mantle in the master bedroom.

Two variations on the theme of three.

*D*etail of the black walnut chiffonier in the

master bedroom, an asymmetrical composition in

ebony, fruitwood, and semi-precious stones.

Chiffonier drawer. A craftsman's hand carved

the wood; an artist's eye first saw the pattern.

V. FLOWERS AND TREES
Bringing Nature to the House

In fact all art loving people love nature first,
then the rest must follow.

Charles Sumner Greene

The Gamble House is situated on a grassy knoll on the east side of Pasadena's arroyo, a broad ravine that forms a natural recreation area known as Brookside Park. The early homes in this neighborhood had a spectacular view of the San Gabriel Mountains to the north, with the San Raphael Hills offering a lower profile to the west and south.

The Gambles were drawn to this environment and the Greenes designed a house that would compliment the rustic setting. Then, to reflect a love of nature, they proceeded to bring flowers and trees to the interiors by creating pictures in wood, metal, art glass, and semi-precious stones.

V. Flowers and Trees: Detail of master bedroom desk.

*T*he first floor guest room features

patterns of a trailing rose.

*F*loral inlay in a leg of the maple desk.

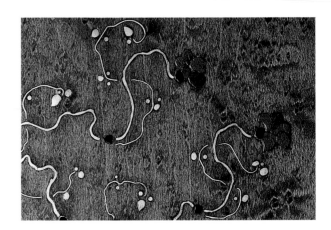

*I*nlay on the door of the letter box is

vermilion wood, ebony and silver.

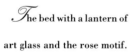

*D*etail of nickel silver bed

in the first floor guest room.

*T*he bed with a lantern of

art glass and the rose motif.

A rose blossoms in the
dining room window.

Detail from the front door. Two layers
of glass create the rich and varied colors.

A copper lamp on the mahogany table in the

entry hall features the Monterey cypress.

*R*edwood panel in the living room, part of a

frieze carved with trees, clouds and birds, is a

variation on the ramma: the open ornamental

work above the sliding screens that form

partitions in a Japanese house.

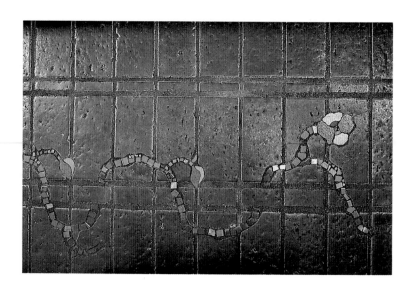

*G*rueby tile in the living room fireplace is

inlaid with a sinuous design of opaque glass.

*E*arth tones form a background for stylized

trees in the living room rug. Squares are

reminiscent of the work of designers Charles

Rennie Mackintosh, Joseph Hoffman and

artist Gustav Klimpt, contemporaries of the

Greenes.

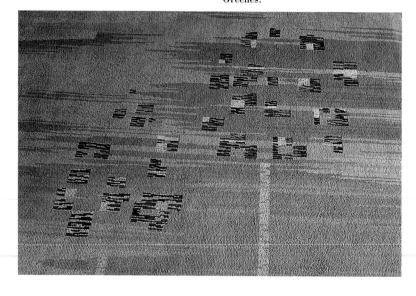

*D*etail of hall lantern near Aunt Julia's bedroom. This seldom noticed treasure with its Japanese pattern blooms in plain sight.

*R*ookwood vase inspired floral inlay in the master bedroom desk.

$\mathcal{D}$etail of black walnut headboard in the master

bedroom. The floral inlay is made of fruitwood and semi-

precious stones. The Japanese forms outlined in ebony

look solid here, but they are open, negative spaces.

VI. DOORS
Studies in Invention

*Doors should be interesting in themselves and
not merely holes of entrance and exit.*

Charles Sumner Greene

Because The Gamble House relates to its surroundings and concentrates on privacy within, it is a house of doors. There are over fifty, all of them distinctly more than "merely holes of entrance and exit."

Exterior doors, often appearing in groups of two or three, feature the oriental lift and are always glass to let in as much light as possible from under the wide eaves. In the entry hall, ten feet of leaded art glass display a gnarled oak tree in rich earth tones that vary with the changing light. The center portal, four feet 7 inches wide, contains the trunk and main branches. The tree dominates the area as it spreads out into the narrower entries at each side and up into the transoms, creating a floor to ceiling composition.

To minimize vertical accents, the door heights throughout are four inches lower than average; the small stature of David and Mary Gamble made six foot four inch openings quite appropriate. In keeping with the strong horizontal emphasis, the lintels continue all the way around each room, and serve as a unifying element.

Doorknobs and middle hinges, are installed above the midpoint. This arrangement adds support to the upper part where it is needed.

With typical regard for detail, Charles Greene turned his creative attention to five wardrobe closets on the second floor. For the storage area of each bedroom and the upstairs hall, he provided a separate, inventive design.

VI. Doors: *G*arage door detail.

Detail of the front doors.

From the entry hall, at dusk.

*P*ocket doors are venerred on
one side with teak to match the
hall, and on the other with
mahogany like the dining room.

*M*ahogany and art
glass door between the
dining room and pantry.

*S*torage cabinets in

the upstairs hall.

A collection of doors in the kitchen,

all of maple, some with glass.

A teak door with iridescent glass

stands open in the dining room hall.

Beyond, a small vestibule leads to

the kitchen and the back stairs.

*W*ardrobe closets

in Aunt Julia's bedroom,

the simplest on the second floor.

*C*loset doors in the master bedroom.

Oak handles are detailed to match the

drawer pulls in the room.

The ray design distinguishes wardrobe

doors in the boys' bedroom.

Storage wall in the upstairs guest room.

*L*eaded art glass doors to the divided bathroom

on the second floor provide privacy for the bath,

light and beauty for the hall.

*P*lating the room side of the door with
opaque white glass, dispatches shadows and
keeps the bathroom uniformly white.

*W*ide glass doors to the rear of the main hall offer a reflection of the terrace and a glimpse of the front door as well.

*T*he garage, a structure worthy of the house, presents distinctive doors of oak with wrought iron hinges extending all the way across.

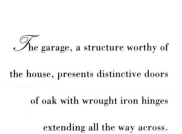

VII. Fireplaces
Variation on a Subject

*A real fireplace does heat and does not smoke.
If it does this much it will be appreciated,
but to be a real joy it must appeal to our love of
the beautiful.*

Charles Sumner Greene

For a residence built with central heating, The Gamble House has an extravagant number of hearths. One was planned for every major room with the exception of the guest areas. It would seem that the Greenes and the Gambles shared Frank Lloyd Wright's conviction that the fireside was the symbol of the home, essential to every house and, if one could afford it, to each important room.

The Greenes designed every fireplace "to be a real joy"; each has its own individuality. Four are faced with Grueby tile inlaid with Tiffany glass, the other two are made of pressed brick. The living room hearth provides for the pleasure of a roaring wood fire. The others are equipped with grates holding ceramic briquettes which were heated by a gas flame until they glowed red and radiated a measure of warmth into the room. Aunt Julia's fireplace hardly qualifies as one, however it is included here because of the tasteful Grueby tile and the handsome mantle with cabinet doors of leaded glass.

VII. Fireplaces: *Detail from dining room andirons.*

$\mathcal{T}$he living room fireplace.

$\mathcal{D}$etail of living

room fireplace with

tools by Greene &

Greene.

$\mathscr{D}$ining room fireplace of Grueby tile.

The extended copper lintel continues the

prevalent horizontal accents in the house.

*T*iffany glass inlay to compliment Mary

Gamble's fern bowl by Tiffany.

*A*ndirons in the dining room

restate the floral motif.

$\mathscr{T}$he den fireplace with Gothic overtones, uses

pressed brick similar to the exterior steps and

terrace borders. Designed without a mantle

because the room is small, it gains interest from

the changing planes and contours.

$\mathscr{F}$ireplace and sitting area in the

master bedroom. The tile is Grueby

with accents of opaque glass.

$\mathscr{A}$ pattern on the andirons restates the

wood inlay motif over the mantle.

$\mathcal{P}$ressed brick and marble mantle in the

boys' room. The abstraction above,

varies the motif in the master bedroom.

$\mathcal{A}$unt Julia's fireplace was modified in

the final plans to serve as a firewall for a

Franklin stove that was never installed.

Behind a pink rosebud in the bouquet is

the "temporary covering" for the flue.

VIII. LEADED ART GLASS
Painting With the Rainbow

*Leaded glass is sometimes used and it is very
effective where it seems to fill a real need.*

Charles Sumner Greene

California bungalows, with their predominant use of wood and earth tones, are known for their monochromatic appearance both inside and out. This tendency is emphasized by the broad, overhanging eaves which shade walls and windows from the harsh sunlight, but create dim interiors at the same time. Accents of color and texture become very important in adding interest and variety to a room. It is not surprising that Persian rugs, art pottery, copper accessories and art glass enjoyed great popularity during the Craftsman Period.

Fortunately, Charles Greene found many places in the Gamble House where leaded glass seemed "to fill a real need". His beautiful designs appear in windows, doors, light fixtures and lanterns. They were crafted by Emil Lange who owned a glass studio in Los Angeles and had worked for Louis Comfort Tiffany in New York.

Most of the stained glass in The Gamble House is from the Tiffany Studios, bringing a luminous beauty to the interiors as it compliments and enriches the various woods. When the light source is primarily from the back, it elicits sunny tones ranging from amber to golden yellow. Strong light from the front creates a dazzling iridescence on the surface of the glass, reminiscent of mother of pearl. These marvelous accents change throughout the day, particularly in the summer, as the sunlight travels from the front doors with their magnificent oak tree, to the west side of the house where slanting rays of afternoon sun transform the living room and dining room with lustrous rainbow colors.

VIII. Leaded Art Glass: *T*errace lantern detail.

Details from the front doors
of leaded Tiffany glass.

Late in the day, iridescent tones

appear in the dining room lantern.

Detail of lantern in the

first floor guest room.

A light transforms the glass.

*W*indow at the foot of the
stairway to the third floor.

*A*n alternative light
source releases new colors.

*D*etail from the dining room window.

*T*he same window begins to change its hues.

*L*ooking toward the fireplace in late afternoon; the dining room light fixture trades amber for cerise and green.

*T*he dining room at night.

*I*nterior view of the front doors at dusk.

The Author

The interest of Jeanette Thomas in education and architecture has influenced her activities as a member of the Docent Council of the Gamble House since 1977. After receiving her bachelor's and master's degrees from Stanford University, she taught social studies and English in California secondary schools and was a member of the faculty of Colorado State College of Education, now the University of Northern Colorado. Ms. Thomas has written materials for the use of visitors touring the Gamble House and for self-guided tours of the surrounding neighborhood, and has developed resources for docent training and the Junior Docent Program which teaches seventh and eighth graders to conduct tours for Pasadena school children. Married to Frank Thomas, veteran Disney animator and author, she is the mother of one daughter and three sons, one of whom photographed *Images of the Gamble House*.

The Photographers

Los Angeles native Theodore Thomas and Tokyo-born Kuniko Okubo have collaborated as filmmakers on award-winning programs for the Disney Channel, PBS, and the National Geographic Television Specials. For Thomas, *Images of the Gamble House* marks a return to his roots as a still photographer. Guided by Jeanette Thomas, he and Okubo planned and executed each of the pictures in this book with an eye to the changing patterns of natural light in the Gamble House at different times of the day. A minimal amount of artificial illumination was employed as needed to augment what the sun provided. The photographs, shot over a four month period during the late summer and fall, are intended to reveal the House as seen by those who have been fortunate enough to live in it.

Initial support for this book was provided by the The Docent Council of the Gamble House, USC; The Gamble House Bookstore, and the many individuals who believed in the project.